DEAD END
OR
DIVINE ENCOUNTER?

To: Ms. Pat
To God be the
glory. Thank you
for your support!

DEAD END
OR
DIVINE ENCOUNTER?

Kevin V. Gresham II

Dead End or Divine Encounter? Discovering Opportunity Through Adversity
2nd Edition

By Kevin V. Gresham II

Cover Design by Nate Baron.

© Copyright 2015

ISBN-10: 1517470005
ISBN-13: 978-1517470005

Printed in the U.S.A.

PRAISE

Soren Kierkegaard said, "Life can only be understood backwards; but it must be lived forwards." This young man who I've known all of his life has captured this quote from Soren in this wonderful book, *Dead End or Divine Encounter*. It is wonderful to see such maturity, at such a young age, as he shares his journey to show others that Psalm 37:23 is indeed true; that the steps of a good man may seem like a *dead end*, but in actuality, they are *divine encounters*. For God not only orders our steps, he also orders our stops.

Rev. Therm James
Senior Pastor, Bethany Baptist Church
Baltimore, MD

"I have watched and observed the life and the development of Kevin Gresham II over the past 20 years. He has developed into a mature and seasoned young man who will have an impact on the kingdom of God. I celebrate him in the writing of his first book and I know his story and sharing will be an encouragement and blessing to many others!"

Rev. John Jenkins
Senior Pastor, First Baptist Church
Glenarden, MD

"Being a close personal friend of Kevin, I've had the privilege of having a front row view of the life-changing events he so candidly speaks about in this book. As I re-live the details collectively with each chapter, I am even more amazed and in awe of the transformation that has taken place in Kevin's life. I never knew the exact principles put in place, but I saw the change first-hand; and I must say, I'm a believer. So if you've found yourself at a dead end in life, this book may just be your Divine encounter."

Derrick Murry
Federal Police Officer
Varsity Quarterback Coach
Riverdale Baptist High School

Kevin's inspirational story is a beacon of light and encouragement. His never give up attitude conveys a timely, spiritual message of hope, unwavering faith, courage, and a determination to succeed. This book exemplifies how God's love for us overshadows all obstacles.

Dr. Linda M. Campbell
Former Secondary Principal
Educational Consultant
Campbell & Associates, LLC

To my parents, Kevin & Denise Gresham

I thank God for blessing me with the greatest dynamic duo of parents on this side of heaven. It's because of you that I did not give up at my dead end and it's also because of you that I was introduced to the Divine. I thank you for never giving up on me and I pray that you will be forever proud.

Contents

Acknowledgments

Callece - I truly do not have words to describe how special you are to me. I have said this before, and I will say it again. The Bible says that a man that findeth a wife, findeth a good thing (Proverbs 18:22). I believe a man that findeth a Callece Gresham, he findeth a GREATER thing. I thank you for your unconditional love and support, but most of all I thank God for exceeding my greatest expectations when he blessed me with you. Love, Hubby

Kallie Vee–The one I affectionately call Daughta Waughta Taughta. You will probably hate that name when you get older but I wrote this book with you in mind. I pray that when you are of age you will learn from daddy's mistakes and be a greater person. I love you and thank God in advance for what He is going to do in your life. Love, Daddy

Mom - The concept of this entire book came from the words that you shared with me. I truly do not have enough room on this page to thank you. I love and appreciate all of the whoopings, punishments, and raised tones (LOL - trying to be euphemistic here) that you directed toward me. Even though those experiences were painful, they were necessary. I love you and thank you for not giving up on me.

Dad - My Hero! There is a story told about a man who grew up seeking dragons because he knew that they were not real. He also sought after fathers because he did not have one. So, he grew up hoping that dragons could be real and fathers could be real.[1] I thank God for the opportunity and privilege to have a father as I was growing up who was not a myth but actually a real person in my household. All I can say is that I love you and thank you for being the best father that anyone could ever ask for.

Dishon - Bro, my prayer is that I have been an inspiration to you. I know that I have not been the best and I could have done more, but please know that I have always had the best intentions. I   thank you for being who you are, and I am praising God for who you are going to be. Love you dearly.

Mr. & Mrs. Clarence Harris & Veronica Toliver (Doll Doll) - Your support has been invaluable. I do not know what I would have done without the many lessons that I have learned from you. Please know that I love you and thank God for you.

Mr. & Mrs. Jack Gresham - Thank you for teaching me legacy. Your love and care before I was born has had a profound impact on me today. Even though I was only able to meet one of you, I thank God for you and love both of you. I pray that as you look over the balcony of eternity you are proud.

Anthony & Sarah Thomas - Words cannot express the appreciation that I have for the people who raised my wife. I will forever be grateful and thankful for your lives. Love, Kev

Greater Saint John Church - I am sorry that I cannot list all the people who have been so supportive of me over the years. Your love and support has been amazing. So, please know from the bottom of my heart that I love and thank each and every one of you.

Dr.(Mrs.)L. Campbell - The high school principal that God used as a catalyst for His glory. I am eternally grateful for your spiritual wisdom and educational presence in my life. You believed in me when most did not. I thank you, and I thank you some more for holding me accountable, encouraging me to choose to make right decisions for my life. I pray the Lord blesses you and your family as a result of your amazing work.

I truly thank all of those who made this book possible: St. Paul Press, Dr. Bobby Manning, copyeditor Yvette Blair-Lavallais, book cover designer Nate Baron, Torrey Smith, the Amatos Family, and the Updegraff Family. I also appreciate those who have served as personal and distant mentors: Marvin Kimbrough (Coach!), The Carroll Family, Bishop Neil C. Ellis, Bishop John Francis, Dr. Howard John Wesley, Dr. Otis Moss III, Dr. Jamal H. Bryant, Pastor Steven Furtick, Pastor Kyle Idleman, Pastor HB Charles Jr., and Pastor Jeffrey Johnson. And finally, those who have served as sources of inspiration: My Kabul, Afghanistan Crew, Min. Rodney Carter Jr., Pastor Reginald Sharpe Jr., Rev. Lesley Francisco, and Rev. Marissa Farrow.

Last but certainly not least, I praise, worship

and bless the name above all names, Jesus, the Christ. Thank you for holding back the things that I deserved and giving me things that I did not deserve. Your grace and mercy have kept me. Thank you for saving my life.

Foreword

Although it has been several years since I met Kevin on the football field during our time at the University of Maryland, College Park, I was unaware of all the prior events that had transpired in his life. I just knew him as a respectable individual, who worked hard and was focused on making something of his career. After reading his book, Dead End or Divine Encounter, however, it proved what I knew of the author was only a small piece of his story. As a man and a professional athlete, I agree that winners are created during times of adversity. I have faced many difficult situations where things were nearly impossible to overcome, but I never allowed the situations to defeat me, which is exactly what Kevin shares about his story. Therefore, this book is not only appropriate to those going through tough times, but also for any individual who wants to succeed. We all face challenging moments during our time on this earth and this book serves as a source of inspiration on the appropriate steps to take when we feel as though we have reached our dead end.

The author relied on God during his troubling times and expressed how those moments served to increase his faith in the Lord. Maybe you are searching for God in your life. Maybe you have already found Him but want to know Him better. In this book, Kevin will help you see the Lord's hand in your life especially in times of trouble. He will teach you that success or failure isn't about avoiding the hard times, but deciding what to do when those hard times come, which is to look to God for direction. Enjoy the book!

Torrey Smith
NFL Super Bowl XLVII Champion
President of the Torrey Smith Foundation

INTRODUCTION
My Dead End

"Trials are unavoidable — but that doesn't mean they have to be unprofitable. When God tests you, it's time to learn another lesson..."[1]

—*Dr. Tony Evans*

It was June of 2002 and my summer break was off to an awesome start of doing what I loved to do, play golf. I had just completed the 10th grade at a private school, when I received a letter. The letter was an academic probation notification. In essence, due to me having a grade point average (GPA) less than a 2.0 during a semester, I was placed on academic probation. I was then expected to improve my gpa in the next quarter or semester, or I would have to withdraw from the school. I cannot say I was in the least bit shocked, but I was a bit disappointed. This letter came as no surprise because it was the second time in the past two years I had received this letter from my high school. Nonetheless, I was disappointed because the chances of enjoying a game of golf that day or for the summer were slim to none. The notion of being asked to withdraw from school, a second time, for the same reason was mind-boggling. However, as I reflect on that summer day, I can honestly say that receiving that letter was one of the greatest moments of my life. It was the moment that my life began to change for the better.

As of right now, you might be wondering where I am going with all of this. More than likely, you are either intrigued and will continue in this reading or you are about to stop reading because you believe it will be a waste of time. For some, it might be. For others, this book will encompass the change you have wanted to see in your own life. Every page of this book depicts how life can turn completely around when the necessary actions are taken to become serious about the change you want to see in your life.

I reference change frequently in this book, but a lot of times change is the result of a dead end situation. The dictionary defines dead end as "an end of a road or passage from which no exit is possible" or "a situation offering no prospects of progress or development."[2] I believe my life on that summer day fits this definition perfectly. I had just failed the 10th grade with a disgustingly low grade point average, I was asked to withdraw from school, my parents were ready to give up on me, and overall I felt like a failure. I was in a very dark place in life and really didn't understand the situation until I received that letter. I had reached a dead end. I felt that I had somewhat run out of chances, with no hope of bouncing back.

Throughout my life, my mother would repeat over and over again, "Kevin, if you don't get your act together you're going to run smack dab into a brick wall." That phrase did not have much influence on this typical teenager who considered homework, reading, and studying the last items on his priority list. Although my parents made tremendous sacrifices for me to attend a private school, I pranced around as if they had a moral obligation to send me because my father was the pastor of a church.

High school marked the start of my semi-real world. The grades earned in high school would be the determining factors for college acceptance, internships, and possible job opportunities. But I was not bothered by any of it, until I hit my dead end. After I was shown tremendous grace by the principal, who readmitted me twice into the same school, I began to ponder why God displayed so much favor in my life. Quite evidently, when you are a child of God, there is a plan and purpose for your life that no one can alter. That's it! When you get to those moments in life when it seems as if you don't have anywhere to go and nowhere to turn, God is standing right there waiting for you to see the good through this bad situation.

More recently during my travels abroad, I attended a service at Ruach City Church in London, England, where Bishop T. D. Jakes was the guest speaker. Bishop Jakes spoke on the topic "When Opportunity Knocks?" Now immediately, I thought God must be the one at the door with a wonderful opportunity. While that answer was not totally false, Bishop Jakes took his point a little deeper than my surface response. The premise behind the message was that opportunities knock on the door of life but it's a matter of whether we open the door and take advantage of the opportunity. God has a way of showing up in many ways. He sometimes shows up through situations that are good and He also shows up through situations that are bad. That is why I firmly believe that whenever you reach your dead end; your place of failure, disappointment, depression, hurt or pain, God stands right there waiting   and hoping that you see him, the life, at your dead end. Dead ends are truly Divine Encounters, meetings that God orchestrates through the circumstances of life to get you to the next stage of your life. The question is, will you see the adverse situation for what it is on the surface or will you come to the spiritual realization that your situation is a life-filled opportunity disguised as a dead end? As a result of God helping me see beyond my failures, my life has never been the same. I went from having one of the lowest GPAs in high school to having the highest GPA (4.0) in my freshman class as a college student athlete. This is just one of the many testimonies that have taken place in my life all because I decided not to die at my dead end. Just as I decided to take advantage of my dead end situation, I believe you can do the same. What path will you choose on this day - death or life? I chose life at my dead end and my prayer is that you will too. Enjoy.

Transcripts - First 2 Years of High School

# COURSE	SM1	SM2	CREDIT
Gresham II; Kevin V	HS 09 #033		
YR: 2000-2001	RANK: 45 of 52		
CR: 6.50	GPA: 1.64		
109 English 9	D-	D	1.00
209 Phy Sci	D-	D-	1.00
309 Algebra 1	C	F	0.50
409 Geography	B-	C-	1.00
514 Bible 9/10	D-	D-	1.00
508 Col Keybrd	C+	B	1.00
922 PE/Health M	B	C+	1.00
AVERAGES:	1.9	1.4	6.50

ATT: ABS: 6.0   TAB: 44.0

# COURSE	LEV	SM1	SM2	CREDIT
Gresham, II; Kevin	GH 10 #033			
YR: 2001-2002	RANK: 43 of 46			
CR: 11.50	GPA: 1.55			
110 English 10	HS	D+	F	0.50
210 Biology	HS	F	D-	0.00
310 Plane Geom	HS	C+	C	1.00
412 US History	HS	F	F	0.00
514 Bible 9/10	HS	B	C-	1.00
720 Spanish 1	HS	C+	F	0.00
936 HS Art	HS	B+	A	1.00
AVERAGES:		1.6	1.3	4.50

ATT: ABS: 0.0   TAB: 22.0

Transcript - First Year of College

Course Id		Title	Grade	Credits	QPnts
		FALL 2004			
ERE001		Rdg Stdy Skills	A	3.00	12.00
gac100		Fresh Orient	A	2.00	8.00
hmu305		Hist Of Jazz II	A	3.00	12.00
MAT002		Elem Algebra	A	3.00	12.00
rec111		Health & Wellness	A	2.00	8.00
rec113		Tennis & Volleyball	A	1.00	4.00

	Attempt	Earned	Total	GPACrd	QPnts	GPA
Term	14.00	14.00	14.00	14.00	56.00	4.00
Cum	14.00	14.00	14.00	14.00	56.00	4.00

Course Id		Title	Grade	Credits	QPnts
		SPRING 2005			
BCA330		Comp Prog/mis	A	3.00	12.00
HEN112		Freshman English I	A	3.00	12.00
HLS101		Elem Span I	A	3.00	12.00
HPH213		Ethics	A	3.00	12.00
MAT111		Intermediate Algebra	A	3.00	12.00
RSW201		Intro To Sociology	A	3.00	12.00

	Attempt	Earned	Total	GPACrd	QPnts	GPA
Term	18.00	18.00	18.00	18.00	72.00	4.00
Cum	32.00	32.00	32.00	32.00	128.00	4.00

End of Transcript

SECTION 1
IDENTIFICATION

CHAPTER 1
Find The Fault

"Truly it is an evil to be full of faults; but it is a still greater evil to be full of them and to be unwilling to recognize them, since that is to add the further fault of a voluntary illusion." [1]

—*Blaise Pascal*

Finding fault within is not always comfortable. Self-assessments have been and will always be one of the most grueling and daunting tasks because they mandate a moment of truth that in many cases is painful. Although identifying faults within can be difficult, it is sometimes the discovery that is needed to get one to the next stage in life.

One of my closest friends, Joseph, founder of BCWellness, has a tremendous weight-loss story. For years, before he made his remarkable turnaround, he didn't want to face the fact that he was overweight. Many years went by and his weight steadily increased.

It wasn't that he didn't know or was unaware of his weight; a physician notified him that he was considered morbidly obese. He was also reminded every morning when he saw himself in the mirror, when co-workers made comments, and when loved ones suggested that he pay attention to his weight. Then one day he boarded a plane and the flight attendant said he needed to purchase an additional ticket because of his weight. This incident was the starting point of his life change. Now he has the testimony of losing over 100 pounds all because he decided to take the first step, facing the fault.

Is it even possible to advance if you never deal with the issues that set you back? What's the possibility of overcoming stumbling blocks without first identifying them as stumbling blocks? Simply put, it is impossible for anyone to succeed in life without taking the necessary first step - facing fault and failure. Once you have identified that, embrace it, learn from it, and move forward.

Story of David

As we discuss the topic of facing faults and failures, I am reminded of a prominent king in the Bible by the name of David. He had an issue with owning up to his mistakes. David was caught in the act of adultery with a woman named Bathsheba. 2 Samuel 11 tells us that King David was a mighty and powerful man who was an awesome leader for the children of Israel. He was the man who was appointed king after King Saul, and he led the Israelites through many battles to victory. One day David saw Bathsheba bathing. He inquired and found that she was married to one of his soldiers. That didn't stop David because his attraction to Bathsheba led him to sleep with her and as a result she was impregnated. However, instead of David facing the fact that he made a mistake and now had an issue on his hands, he conspired to kill Bathsheba's husband, Uriah, and then married Bathsheba to cover up his sin. All of these things were done while he was the king and spiritual advisor of Israel. Some time had passed and Bathsheba gave birth to a son. During this extended period of time, David did not come to grips with his sin until the prophet of the Lord, Nathan, went to him one day and presented a scenario about him, without telling him that he was the subject of the story. The prophet told the story and concluded that there was a good and bad character. David spoke up after the prophet finished and said that the bad character in the story should be punished and should not receive pity for his sins. The prophet then laid the hammer down on David, saying, "You are the man!" After hearing the word from the prophet, David realized that he had to face this issue from his past.

According to Psalm 51:3, David's sin during this incident was at the forefront of his mind often. The sinful nature of David's past presented a major mental blockade. The Scriptures do not say what took place in that time, but there is the possibility that these thoughts not only affected David mentally and spiritually, but may also have affected him socially and physically. Many times in life we have David moments. We encounter issues from our past that we did not handle; instead, we covered them up and they became toxic for growth in all areas of our lives so much so that we are not even cognizant of how wrong our actions really are until they are brought to our attention by those around us.

This is the same thing that happened to me in my first year of high school. After receiving the first academic probation withdrawal letter, I was fully aware that I had failed and that my academic career was off to a horrible start. My drive and passion for success academically was a problem, and it needed to be addressed. As a result of not dealing with the problem, it grew worse. I received a second withdrawal letter in the mail the following year but, it took my principal's final letter to get me to realize that I needed to change. As we can learn from David and my personal story, it is imperative to face our personal issues and recognize the fault within ourselves instead of having those around us identify it for us.

The enemy uses invisible bricks

When we disregard our past and present issues, we allow the enemy to spiritually create and build brick walls in our lives to prevent us from moving forward. The more we avoid them, the more of a stronghold they establish and the harder they are to overcome. Inwardly, this is where the enemy wins the battle because he gets us to the point where we have avoided our issues so successfully that we become oblivious to having a problem. This is why I believe the enemy uses invisible bricks to erect walls in our lives that make us believe we are progressing, while in reality, we are holistically unproductive. The invisible brick wall that stands in our path of life presents the illusion of a road ahead. As time passes, we do not feel that change is needed because it seems as if our issues have not affected us. On this road, it seems that we are still moving, living, eating, and paying bills. Ultimately, it appears that we are still operating even though things in our past and present are unresolved.

Many of us fall victim to running into a brick wall at some point in our life. King David, the previously mentioned king of Israel, had a brick wall moment but he finally came around and realized that he had been doing evil in the sight of God and never repented for his faults or asked God for forgiveness. In Psalm 51, David finally identifies the brick wall, his issue. So, through prayer, he asks God to renew his spirit and remove the sin in his life that was holding him hostage. Essentially, David recognized that he had a problem, and with that subtle but profound encounter, that recognition changed the rest of his life.

Is this your situation? Are you allowing your past to weigh you down? Are you allowing previous mistakes to taunt you? Do you have parasitic issues that have never been dealt with and as a result have caused you to become stagnate? If so, you are in the perfect position for God to turn your situation around. Identification is the key starting point to finding hope in life. We cannot handle our own issues. We need to recognize that we are not the Almighty. We are finite and sinful beings who are not independent of but rather dependent on the infinite and sovereign God. Just as you saw in the story of David, once David realized and identified himself as the inferior one, the superior One had room to work in his life. As a result, the Lord blessed David because of his sincere and honest assessment. Before David went to the Lord, he suffered major consequences. He was mentally frustrated, damnation came to his family, his son died, and his family was cursed. However, after he prayed, acknowledged, and identified his wrong, the Lord blessed him with the wisest man of all, a son named Solomon.

It is okay to have areas in our lives that need help. However, it is not permissible to have problems that need to be identified or have been identified, but yet nothing is done. Meg Gay argues in her book, *The Defining Decade* that this current social media society is psychologically problematic for this generation; it forces people to believe that they must be perfect. User profiles on Twitter, Facebook, IG (Instagram), Tumblr, and other social streams portray people as living picture-perfect lives[2] when in reality their lives are just like everybody else's, filled with ups and downs. This inevitably forces people to run away from their issues because they do not feel sufficiently comfortable to confront and embrace them. Ultimately, the only way to advance in life is to address the things that are blocking our path to success; only then can we move forward without falling victim to living life in a constant state of oblivion. While many believe that identifying faults and failures is unimportant, I believe that it is necessary because it is truly the first step in discovering the path to destiny.

CHAPTER 2
But I Have Done Nothing Wrong!

"In the final analysis, the questions of why bad things happen to good people transmutes itself into some very different questions, no longer asking why something happened, but asking how we will respond, what we intend to do now that it happened." [1]

—*Pierre Teilhard de Chardin*

It is understood that some people live in a constant state of oblivion and believe that they are never in the wrong, never have issues, or never have done anything that would be looked upon as negative. My father would often say that people who feel as if they are perfect and always speak in heavenly language, people who are never caught speaking about anything other than God, are so spiritual that they are spooky. Romans 3:23 states, "For all have sinned and have fallen short of the glory of God." No one on the earth is faultless. I believe that the lessons the Lord is trying to teach through the dead ends in life will not always hinge on our bad decisions or sins. Sometimes God places expiration dates on a particular season of life and sends us a sign that it is time to move on. This means that identification is not always focused on finding the fault or issues that hinder our progress but, in all actuality, identification can be argued as discovering Christ's direction in everything.

The dead end that you are facing in life may not be a past issue or a committed sin. It may be a poor and unproductive mentality, a bad friendship, or the end of a professional career. This type of dead end is sometimes the most difficult issue to identify and confront because it is not always the most apparent. Many of us directly associate negative outcomes with sinful practices. However, as we discover in the life of Job, who lived a blameless life yet his health, wealth, and family were taken away from him, bad things can happen to good people. Understand that the negative things that occur in someone's life are not necessarily connected to sin. Many of you will experience dead ends in life simply because the Lord is directing you on a new path. In other words, your assignments in certain areas of life (e.g., church ministry, professional life, circle of friends) have an expiration date. Therefore, the Lord finds a way to get you to see that your time on this road has ended and that it's time to move in a different direction. It is for this reason that many who experience this sort of situation might wonder:

Why is nothing at work going right anymore?
Why have I separated from certain friends, family members, co-workers, or associates?
Why has my tolerance for foolishness changed?
Why have my desires for life changed?
Why have I simply felt the need for total change?

Perhaps God has created a dead end in your life and He is looking for you to find Him in the situation to discover your true direction and purpose, which is what happened to Job. Even though he lost everything, he endured the test of not giving up on God, and in the end God blessed him with more than he ever had before.

This dead end won't move

When I wrote this book, I was living in London, England with my family. Those who have visited

London or ever lived in a busy and congested city know that road closures are pretty common. In my neighborhood, the local construction workers put up a sign in the road that said "Dead End" to denote that all cars coming down that road would eventually get stuck and have to turn around. Normally, the workers place these signs in certain streets leading to the construction site that has shut down the road, but sometimes they forget to warn you and you end up finding the dead end by yourself. After a while, the construction workers complete their task and eventually the road is reopened. Nonetheless, these experiences are annoying because they prevent people from going down a road that they are comfortable with or a road that they believe is needed for travel to their desired destination.

Spiritually, this is where I believe God steps in. Unlike the construction site that will eventually be complete and the road that used to lead to a dead end will be reopened, some dead ends that God places in our lives are meant to stay. Many times we believe that the obstacles we face in life must be moved. However, what if the Lord divinely decides for you to travel to that dead end? What if God ordains for you to continue to walk down that road so that you finally get to a place where you are dependent upon Him? What if God sets up a dead end, a disappointment, or depressing circumstance in your life to finally get you to meet Him? While we are praying for certain obstacles to be removed, God is trying to teach us something: Some obstacles will never be moved. Therefore, don't be surprised if God speaks in your spirit and says, "The road that you have been traveling down, with a career path, with a cherished relationship, with a church, or even with a habit, has come to an end. There is no more road left to travel with that situation, with those people, or with those thoughts." Legal authorities use the phrase "cease and desist," which means to stop all activities or else corrective actions will be taken.

I often feel that it is important to have a solid spiritual connection so that we can perceive the Spirit's presence in every situation. The children of God are spiritual beings designed to fulfill the plan and purpose of the Father. This cannot be achieved if God does not reveal Himself to us; sometimes the only way He can do that is by allowing us to run smack dab into trouble, where there is nowhere else to turn.

CHAPTER 3
Spiritual Dead Ends

The biggest threat to the church today is fans - enthusiastic admirers, who call themselves Christians but aren't actually interested in following Christ. Fans often confuse their admiration for devotion. They mistake their knowledge of Jesus for intimacy with Jesus.[1]
—Kyle Idleman

While it can be argued that identifying dead ends in our professional careers is important, I would contend that identifying spiritual dead ends in our spiritual lives is more important. In 2011, I purchased a book written by Kyle Idleman, entitled *Not a Fan*. The only reason I purchased the book was because of its intriguing title[22]. I really had no idea of the book's premise nor had I ever read any of the author's books in the past. Little did I know that God would orchestrate me reading a book in order to change my whole perspective on Christianity and literally walk me down the road to salvation again.

The book helped me realize that during this so-called Christian journey I was on I had only made a decision to "believe" in Christ, but had never made a commitment to "follow" Christ. This discovery I learned was the difference between night and day because a verbal decision to believe is distinctively different than a physical commitment to walk in that belief. The Gospel writer in the New Testament, Matthew, records these words of Jesus in chapter seven when he speaks to His disciples during His famous "Sermon on the Mount." Jesus says,

21. Not everyone who says to me, 'Lord, Lord,' will enter the kingdom of heaven, but only he who does the will of my Father who is in heaven. 22. Many will say to me on that day, 'Lord, Lord, did we not prophesy in your name, and in your name drive out demons and perform many miracles?' 23. Then I will tell them plainly, 'I never knew you. Away from me, you evildoers!'

Notice in the 21st verse the distinction between those who SAY and those who DO; note that the two are polar opposites.

This was the case with my own life. While

reading *Not a Fan*, I felt like the author knew my name, address, and history. It was as if he knew what my so-called Christian experience encompassed. I made a decision to believe in Jesus Christ at the early age of nine. I walked down the aisle as many people in the church do and was asked to repeat Romans 10:9 as the pastor said it. Following the scripture, I was told "that if you confess with your mouth Jesus is Lord, and believe in your heart that God raised him from the dead, you will be saved." However, I never embraced what living the life that Christ wanted me to live truly meant. Up until that point, I had adopted all of the faith principles that my parents, Sunday-school teachers, grade-school Bible professors, and fellow church members instilled in me. I followed all the rules to the best of my ability. I thought that not drinking, smoking, indulging in sexual activity, or any of the other major sins mentioned in the Word, were the keys to being a good Christian.

Needless to say, I was wrong. Now I would be lying if I led you to believe that I was perfect, but my personal goal was to follow the guidelines that were set for Christians to follow. In essence, this book helped me realize that following the rules does not mean you are following Jesus. Christianity has nothing to do with adopting the faith of others or doing what you think is best based on traditional religious practices. Christianity is about embracing a life-filled and authentic relationship with Christ, which can include the rules but is also inclusive of following Him in every area and aspect of your life.

Do you have an authentic relationship with Christ? Is your connection to Christ dependent on a neighbor, friend, parent, or pastor? Are you one who has made a decision to believe or a commitment to follow? If you find yourself not being able to confidently answer these questions, you might be in the same place I was, a spiritual dead end. Initially, I felt that coming to this realization about myself was horrible. I was a youth leader, teaching Bible study classes, and doing the work of Christ. But to my surprise, I was not even close to where I thought I was or where I needed to be. As a matter of fact, I thought I was going full speed forward only to realize that I was running in place. That is why I am so glad that I came to this realization; if I had not, I would have delayed my assignment in life. As a result of this major encounter, I have accepted my call to preach the Gospel, started Christian Bible studies in Afghanistan and London, am currently working on my Master of Divinity degree, and have led many to embrace an authentic relationship with Christ.

Hopefully, this chapter has either confirmed

your relationship with Christ or led you to realize that there is work to be done in your relationship with Him. Maybe your issue at this time is not knowing whether you have a relationship with Christ, but gauging the depth of your relationship knowledge of Him versus intimacy with Him. Regardless, everyone's relationship with Christ can use a check-up every now and then. The question just becomes, what do you do after the issues have been revealed? Ultimately, dead ends can appear in many different ways, but the identification stage is the first door that God wants His children to walk through to reach our Divine destiny.

SECTION 1
Application

1. Take time to pray for clarity on the things that are keeping you from progressing, growing, and moving forward. Consider asking someone that you trust to give you honest feedback about yourself. They will potentially help you identify issues and problems that need to be addressed.

2. Take a piece of paper and create two lists side-by-side. On the first list, write down your current goals, and on the other list write down your deficiencies, problems, or unaddressed issues. This exercise should expose the reasons why you are not on pace to achieving your goals or will assist in finding ways to achieve your goals faster so that you can create new goals.

3. If you are in a position where you know what your problem is but you simply do not want to give it up, think of your child or loved one struggling in their daily life with that issue. What would you share with them? Try having this conversation with yourself to get your mind thinking of the penalty of staying bound to your problem.

4. If you are currently living the statement of "Bad things happen to good people", stay true to the lifestyle that you know is right. Continue to make good decisions. Pray for spiritual understanding of why these things have happened, seek encouraging outlets that will keep you from getting depressed, and stay close to positive people. This positive reinforcement will help you not to do anything that will make your situation worse.

5. Read the story of David and Bathsheba in 2 Samuel 11-12 out of the Message (MSG) Bible, for an understanding of why identifying the things that are keeping us from moving forward in our lives are better realized sooner rather than later.

6. Consider reading the book, "Failing Forward" by John Maxwell for an understanding of how our mistakes can be turned into stepping stones for success.

SECTION 2
IMPLEMENTATION

CHAPTER 4
You Must Be Intentional

"Growth Doesn't Just Happen. We don't improve by simply living. We have to be intentional about it. And the sooner you make the transition to becoming intentional about your personal growth, the better it will be for you, because growth compounds and accelerates as you remain intentional about it." [1]

—*John Maxwell*

In the process of transition, you must understand that the success of your transition is highly predicated on your true intentions. I have heard many people speak about desiring change for their life, praying for change, or even declaring that change will come. Yet, over time, I find that those people end up in the same exact place. Why is that? Why is it that people who want change and are confident about changing never actually change? I believe it comes down to intention.

According to the *New Oxford American Dictionary*, the definition of intent is to be "determined to do (something)" or "showing earnest and eager attention" to something[22]. In other words, if there is true intent, one has made a decision to devote a tremendous amount of time, is willing to put in a great deal of effort, and is ultimately insistent on accomplishing a desired task.

What I have discovered is that many will make the decision to change mentally but never make the decision to change physically. However, a person must be intentionally willing to make the decision to change both physically and mentally. Too many of us have great ideas but don't have the plan of action to back them up. I once heard the saying, "the road to hell is paved with good intentions." A different way of stating this would be that hell is filled with good intentions, but Heaven is filled with good works. While I don't wholeheartedly agree with the saying, the premise behind it is true. What good is it to have good ideas or good intentions that are only mental exercises chained to the walls of the mind? The intent to change must be lived. We must be the change that we desire to see or else we will stay in a continued state of mediocrity, never achieving but steadily dreaming.

Be intentional about planning

When I was getting ready to make my major transition to a new way of living in the 11th grade, I sat down and began to think about all the things I needed to do to make this change. I took plenty of time to plan out all that the change would entail. This included many sessions of writing a detailed list of ideas that I would need to incorporate into my daily routine. The list that I created was long, tedious, and grueling to bring to reality due to the fact that I mentally skipped the 8th - 10th grades. For all the lessons taught during those years I had to make a plan to somehow revisit them to move on to the 11th grade. Regardless of how long the exercise took and how difficult it was to come to grips with my past failures, I was determined to be intentional about the change I wanted to see.

This was not an easy process. I literally had to go against my will every day. Whenever I felt the urge to take breaks and relax, I did the opposite and forced myself to work. Whenever I received a call from a friend to hang out or talk for long periods of time, knowing that I had work to accomplish, I did the opposite. Theoretically, I made a tremendous effort to force positive and productive habits into my life until they became routine and second nature. This strategy helped me tangibly combat the spirit of complacency that I had developed in my past.

While it is important to spend time in thought, it is also important to make the mental decision to plan for the future. I believe that it is even more important to make a decision to physically take action on those plans to see them come to fruition. Being intentional about your decision for change is a key step in implementing a winning strategy to change.

CHAPTER 5

~~Go Hard or Go Home~~

Go NOW Or Go Home!

"Change does not roll in on the wheels of inevitability,
but comes through continuous struggle. And so we must
straighten our backs and work for our freedom.
A man can't ride you unless your back is bent."[1]
—*Martin Luther King, Jr.*

I have discovered a growing problem in the world. The problem is that people believe they have time to get themselves together. The first problem with this is that it's not physically possible to get yourself together. In fact, those in constant pursuit of this will die trying. Spiritually, one cannot get oneself together because Christ is in ultimate control and is the only one who can make all things work in our lives. The second problem with this thought is that you really don't have time to get yourself together. The time to move forward and jump on another path in life is not some distant time from now. The time is now.

The Bible says in Mark 13:32, "no man knows the day or hour" of when anything will happen in life. No one can predict death, sickness, depression, accidents, world tragedies, or many other things that negatively affect our lives. Therefore, take advantage of the fact that you are alive and have the ability right now to make a difference in your life. John Maxwell, leadership guru and author of *Today Matters: 12 Step Daily Practices to Guarantee Tomorrow's Success*, believes that many people in the world look at their daily life in the wrong perspective. He states that we exaggerate yesterday, overestimate tomorrow, and ultimately underestimate our today. Life is made by our daily decision to make the most out of today[2]. Therefore, we have no time to waste thinking that we will have plenty of time tomorrow, next year, in our 30s-50s, or even in our senior seasoned years to get started on doing what we know we need to do now. Today is the key to making success a reality.

Go now before you lose something

I am reminded of the story of Jonah. God

instructed him to go speak to the people of Nineveh.

However, Jonah decided that was not what he wanted to do. He wanted to avoid the route that God wanted him to take at all costs. So, he traveled down a different road to catch a boat to a city named Tarshish. As a consequence of this disobedience, God taught Jonah a lesson. He sent a fish to eat Jonah after a tumultuous storm when Jonah was thrown into the sea. While Jonah was in the belly of the fish for three days and three nights, he realized that he had messed up. So, he prayed to God, honored God, and worshipped God. As a result, the Lord showed mercy on him by delivering him from the belly of the fish and ultimately saving his life. The Bible says in Jonah 3: 1-3, "Then the word of the Lord came to Jonah a second time:2 'Go to the great city of Nineveh and proclaim to it the message I give you.'3 Jonah obeyed the word of the Lord and went to Nineveh." Isn't that funny? The very place that Jonah could have gone initially was the same place that he ended up going.

Does God have to punish us through every circumstance and situation that we experience in life? Could it be that we decide to change the things that we need to change, do the things that we need to do, and be the people that we need to be before trials and tribulations come? Don't misunderstand me.

I believe that there is glory in your story. God molds us and shapes us through our many trials. In fact, I am writing this book as a result of my own failures. However, we sometimes go through things in life simply because we are chasing the easy way out and forsaking the big picture. We allow ourselves to choose the way that is less difficult, the way that is more glamorous, the way that requires no sacrifice, or the way that satisfies popular opinion over the paths that lead to true development toward our purpose.

Go Now! Don't wait until God has to send you through several trials and tribulations before you finally understand that change is needed. Your Jonah experience might not be to lie in the belly of a fish for several days and nights. Your Jonah experience could be to go through divorce, go through illness, experience rejection, lose a job, or even face death. Whatever it is, God has given you the chance to move on whatever change it is that you need to make today. Seize the moment in the moment of opportunity so that you can move one step closer to your destiny. Don't fall for the misconception of believing that you will always have time. The time is now. Go now so that your tomorrow can benefit from the steps you are willing to take today.

CHAPTER 6
You're Good Enough!

"I am incomplete from the top of my head to the soles of my feet, but I am pieces of the Master so they call me a Masterpiece."[1]

—*Paul Tillich*

When I was a child, my father instilled in me the same words that his father instilled in him when he was a child. He would say, "Kevin, you can be anything you want to be. The key to it all is hard work, because hard work always pays off." At the time when I was dealing with my most difficult circumstance academically, I disagreed. I often reflected on Moses's experience with the Lord at the burning bush in Exodus 3. As a result of his insecurity about himself, he told the Lord that he was inadequate and incapable of fulfilling the assignment of leading God's people out of the hands of slavery. Like Moses, I felt the same way about my life. At times, I thought that I was incompetent and lacked the necessary skills to do great things in life, especially since I was faced with such a horrible academic background, I thought it would be impossible for me to recover.

These feelings were not just internally generated but were spoken quite frequently by others. People would often laugh at my report cards or say degrading things to me that destroyed my self-esteem. Even several teachers would chime in and agree with the students. I specifically remember overhearing one conversation; the person said, "It was unanimously decided that the award for Least Likely to Succeed in life goes to Kevin Vincent Gresham II."

I would be lying if I said these words did not hurt, because they did. But I would also be lying if I said that these words did not help. During my freshman year of college, I was on a mission. I had just finished graduating from high school with a scholarship to a Historically Black University in Pennsylvania. I was excited to start school because I knew that I would finally be enrolled in a school where no one knew me as the "F-boy" for having bad grades. So, I started the semester with a bang.

Whenever the teacher gave an assignment, I would begin to work on it that night. My new mentality was that if I was always ahead, I would never be behind. I needed to always repeat that statement to motivate me to turn assignments in and study early for exams. This plan actually started working. I used to go above and beyond so much so that I would meet the teacher every time he/she offered office hours, request additional office hours for additional help, and turn in assignments weeks in advance to get the teacher's feedback before they were due. I must say that if you are a college student or know any college students currently in school, that information is invaluable.

As a result of that strategy, I became a distinguished student, earning multiple president awards in my first year in college. However, the one accolade that made all the difference came from my first English professor. She saw the type of effort and work that I was producing. So, one day during her office hours, as I was getting ready to have her look over a completed project that wasn't due for a month, she said, "Son, you do not belong here. You need to go to a major select university, like a University of Pennsylvania, Penn State, or somewhere else where you can be academically challenged even more than you are here." It was then that I noticed I was beginning to make a new life for myself. For the last five years of my life, I had been considered no good and dumb, but a good athlete. What many considered as the typical African American boy. But thank God for that freshman English teacher because she is the one who truly confirmed that I was changed and was ultimately good enough. The following year I gained enough courage to put in an application to attend one of the top schools in the country for my major, the University of Maryland, College Park, and I was accepted. In my first semester, I became an academic standout by achieving Dean's List honors while walking on to the Maryland Terrapin football team.

Those words along with other things motivated me to become the person I was meant to be. It is now 10 years after graduating at the very bottom of my high school class, and I now have classmates who graduated high school and college with me, asking for job opportunities, asking for job advice, or simply looking up to me for wisdom and encouragement. That is why I thank God for allowing my father to sow those seeds of encouragement into my spirit during my childhood; those were the same words I relied on when I needed them the most.

The Bible declares in Ephesians 3:20, "Now to him who is able to do immeasurably more than all we ask or imagine, according to his power that is at work within us." We know that He can do anything but do we exercise the authority that we have within us? I believe many people miss the power of this verse because they shout too quickly at the first clause. The fact that God is able to do immeasurably more than all we can ask or imagine is powerful, but it is already known and understood. That message has been preached all throughout Scripture. However, the true purpose of this verse is to help readers understand that all the power and authority of God rests within us. That is why God will remain limited and powerless in our lives until we release our faith to let Him be limitless and all-powerful through our lives. Paul writes this verse to the church of Ephesus not only to be intentionally redundant about God's sovereign ability, but also to be empowering about our human capability.

Reach for it!

The woman with the issue of blood is a wonderful example of faith put into action. In the Gospel of Luke, we learn that this was a woman who struggled for 12 long years with an illness. She visited many physicians about her illness and spent all that she had traveling from place to place, but still did not receive her healing. One day she heard about a man named Jesus, and from that moment she pushed to receive her healing, knowing that He could do it. I am sure that she faced much criticism from the people of that day. As a matter of fact, she was considered ceremonially unclean because of the type of disease she carried. No one wanted to be around her or touch her. But that did not stop her because the text lets us know that she pressed her way through the crowd and touched the hem of Jesus' garment and was miraculously healed. I believe that the healing process was not just in the touch but also in the pursuit. When she made the faith decision to physically search, seek, press, and finally reach for Jesus, the healing process began. Touching his garment just completed the healing process. What assures us that this is true is that Jesus says to the woman, "Daughter, your faith has healed you. Go in peace" (Luke 8:48).

What I love most about this story is that this woman reached from her deprived, depressed, and diseased state to her place of deliverance. And it was all because she had the faith to reach beyond her circumstances. Many times, people sit and wait for blessings to come to them, praying and fasting for their change to meet them. However, God says, "While you are waiting on me, I am waiting on you." I believe that Jesus could have easily pursued this woman, just like he visited Jairus' daughter in the very same chapter of Scripture. However, I believe He wanted to see how badly this woman wanted her healing. What was she willing to give up, what was she willing to go through, and what was she willing to endure to receive what she wanted from Jesus? The woman pursued her healing by reaching for what was said to be impossible.

You are good enough. Believers must be more confident in their God-given ability and walk in the assurance that nothing is impossible for those who believe. Don't allow the critics of this world to deter you from what God has intended for you. In this process of working on the steps needed to embrace God's Divine plan, know to not put limits on yourself or God because if God is truly able to do anything, then He is able to do anything through you.

SECTION 2
Application

1. Write out your goals for the year. If you have never done this before, start small by writing out weekly or monthly goals until your confidence in achieving them builds up.

2. Pray, think, and write out tangible steps to complete those goals.

3. Take the time to study four (4) stories of great men or women that you admire and note any positive similarities in their stories. Then also take note of any mistakes they have made and how they recovered from them. Learn and glean from their stories.

4. Think of something that you have always wanted to do. Set a goal and create a plan to

accomplish it this month.

5. Find someone that you know is successful and ask what their daily routine consists of. Take note of what you learn and consider applying those practices to your daily life. Exposure is sometimes the greatest form of education.

6. Consider reading the book, "Today Matters" by John Maxwell, to get an idea of why implementing a strategy for change or success must happen now, today, while you have the opportunity.

SECTION 3
INSPIRATION

CHAPTER 7
Discover Your Y

"The two most important days in your life are the day you are born and the day you find out why." [1]
—*Mark Twain*

One of the most powerful questions that can be asked in life is, WHY? That question is so powerful that it can be coupled with any question anyone ever asks. While it sometimes bothers me to hear people question my reasoning for doing things, it is a pretty pertinent and profound question that informs the person asking the question about the methodology behind my thoughts or actions.

I often ask myself the following: Why am I here? Why am I alive? Why do I feel the need to change? Why now? I believe asking yourself or someone else these questions forces you to explain the notion of purpose. What is the purpose of doing whatever you are doing? What is the purpose of achieving whatever you are trying to achieve? This is what I believe is the key to staying inspired. Not having an answer to the question of why, not having a true understanding of your purpose in doing whatever you are attempting to do, will only lead you down a road that is unsustainable.

In my last year as a Maryland Terrapin football player, I had a decision to make. Was I going to continue playing college football in an attempt to make the NFL or was I going to pursue my passion for people in the business world? Many argued me down for even thinking about leaving the football team, considering my talent and the exposure that the team afforded. I was not a star by any means, but I had played in games, broke the school's all-time record for vertical jump (42.5 ft.), and was one of the top players with the lowest shuttle run speed (3.9). A lot more is needed to make the NFL, but I had key attributes that would potentially help me receive NFL scouting notice. The reality though, is that I did not feel passion for the sport. So, I had to ask myself the question, Why? Why was I playing football? Then I realized that my first full season of playing football was in the 12th grade, and I only started playing to earn a scholarship and because I could beat the guy in front of me athletically. This informed me that there was no rooted passion in me to play the sport; it was simply a potentially lucrative hobby.

I decided to leave the team to pursue my passion for people by securing a job utilizing my finance degree from the Robert H. Smith Business School at the University of Maryland. While many opposed my decision to quit and some still do to this day, I responded by telling them that I had to make the decision for myself. I didn't want to live life going after something someone else wanted me to achieve more than I did. I realized that at the end of the day what was going to sustain me was something I had a personal passion and purpose to do, and not the opinions of other people. If I had gone along trying to please people, I might have been hurt or severely injured trying to fulfill someone else's desire. That is why I am thankful for my decision to go after what I wanted for my life. Now God has blessed me with a job that has allowed my family and me to travel and live in different countries and experience more than we could ever have imagined.

Is the pit close enough?

I have discovered that life drives change in different ways. Another way that I was pushed to make a difference in my life and to seriously change was through envisioning my life as a failure. I have discovered that the reason why we sin is because the pit, danger, is not close enough to affect us. We believe that if we sin or when we sin, the immediate consequences will be delayed or may never surface. That mentality gets us nowhere because the ultimate reason for not sinning, should be to please God. Nevertheless, the concept applies with a mentality to succeed.

During my time of failure, I knew that the consequences of my actions were not immediate. This became evident when I was re-admitted to my high school after I was asked to withdraw the first time in the 9th grade, being in violation of the school's GPA requirement. So, when I started to change, I began to routinely think about how my future would look if I continued to fail. This was inclusive of thoughts about the immediate implications that a failed career would have on my future family. In the end, this helped me and encouraged me to stay on track. I realized that if I kept the harsh reality of potential failures in view, I would feel more compelled to take advantage of every opportunity I had to succeed.

Do you know why you want to change? Do you know the purpose of your desire to move forward in life? Answering these questions is one of the most crucial steps in the process of change. It is important because when you get to a point where you feel like giving up, throwing in the towel, or running away from your new path, your WHY is what will keep you from quitting.

CHAPTER 8
It's Not About You

"We love others best when we love God most."[1]

—Kyle Idleman

In the process of discovering the reasons why I needed to turn my life around, I had an epiphany. The thought of changing my life around just for me didn't seem sufficient. It had to be deeper than that. It was then that I realized I needed to change to benefit others. Isn't that what ultimately matters? Not what you only do for yourself, but what you do for others? What good is it to have great knowledge and many accomplishments, if not to share with others?

Once I began to think specifically about others, the first people who came to my mind were my parents. I had done so horribly in school that I felt responsible for allowing my family name to be associated with foolishness. My family was a huge proponent of education. Both of my parents went to college and worked very hard in life to create a name for themselves. I, on the other hand, was definitely not contributing in a positive way. My grades were a poor reflection of the lessons that my parents instilled in me and the example that was set before me. So, in my mind, it was embarrassing for my parents because I went to a Christian school that was near the church my father pastored. In addition, my father had preached several chapel services at the school in the past and pastored the parents of some of the students who attended the school. Then, outside of school, my parents were faced with questions concerning my poor situation.

On several occasions, I remember guest pastors coming to my church asking about me. My father would respond with glaring remarks about my athletic ability. Then the guest pastor would ask how I was doing academically. My father would first shake his head in disappointment then quickly make light of the situation by saying, "But he is a great athlete." Neglecting to even comment because it was not worth mentioning. Over the years, this was very painful for me to witness but not painful enough for me to change. But once I decided to change, I knew that one of my goals was to make sure that my parents would never be seen in a negative light again.

Secondly, I realized I needed to change to benefit the quality of life for my future family. At that time, I felt like I was on a roll because I was only in the 11th grade; however, I believed then that I needed to begin to plan for how I wanted my family to live, what I wanted them to have, and what legacy I wanted to leave for them. Now many would think that it might be too early for one to think like that, but I disagree. I have learned that the earlier you get your mind wrapped around where you want to go in life, the more focused you will be on the daily path of life. As the recipient of a tremendous upbringing, whose parents exposed me to many of the wonderful things and places in life, I wanted to do the same for my family and more. If I ended up being a deadbeat, incompetent, or lazy man, my family would not be able to reap anything but lessons on what not to do. Therefore, my future family became my motivation to change.

In all humility, I thought I was doing well because I was not being selfish with my motivation to change. I didn't just want cars, clothes, and cash; I wanted more for my life. I was thinking beyond my personal satisfaction and looking into my future unselfishly. However, God revealed to me that my approach was wrong. Yes, that I thought about someone other than myself was good, but it was not the key. God is ultimately my source of motivation for change. Nothing more, nothing less.

God - One of many or one and only?

God, above all things, should be your motivation. If He is not the reason, then the things that you use as motivation will not sustain you when you need them most. Many times, we place God in the midst of our plans and not solely as our planner. I discovered that Christ is not only supposed to be the first one that you seek when looking for answers in life, but He is supposed to be the only one. In the book, *Not a Fan*, the author Kyle Idleman writes that Christ should not be your one of many things in life, but He should be your one and only[2]. This concept is explained through the Word of God. The Bible declares in Matthew 6:33, "But seek first his kingdom and his righteousness, and all these things will be given to you as well." In other words, everything that we need, desire, can have, will have, and have ever had are in Him. Therefore, the reason I began to do better in life was that I discovered the voice of God in my life. And it was through His voice that He revealed unto me the power of Jeremiah 29:11, "For I know the plans I have for you," declares the Lord, "plans to prosper you and not to harm you, plans to give you hope and a future." Isn't that great! That lets us know that we have a God that knows us and has things stored up for us. While many people shout, get happy, and run all over churches because of that verse, the real lesson and call to action comes in verses 13-14, "Then you will call upon me and come and pray to me, and I will listen to you. You will seek me and find me when you seek me with all your heart. I will be found by you," declares the Lord, "and will bring you back from captivity." Now that is shouting material! This lets us know that when we pray to God and seek God not only will we prosper, we can rest assured that when we get lost, He will find us.

So don't be consumed with trying to figure out everything yourself. Know that God is the sustainer of everything. If you seek Him, you will find Him because He is looking for you. Trust and know that He cares and wants the best for your life. As Christians, we must be available to be found. Once that happens, you will understand that it's not about you but about Him working through you.

CHAPTER 9
ALONE Is Not A Curse Word

"Two roads diverged in a wood, and I—I took the one less traveled by, and that has made all the difference." [1]
—*Robert Frost*

I discovered that once I took this new road of change for success, my friend circle changed. Now, to be honest, initially this fact was inevitable. My grades were so bad that I had to go to summer school and repeat courses the following year. My friends and associates at the time all passed their courses and moved on to higher level classes. Second, my circle changed because I was so far behind that I had to learn how to do everything properly. My reading comprehension levels were so low they were embarrassing. I didn't even want to be around certain people because my weaknesses would be exposed. Then, finally, once I made a decision for Christ to be the head of my life, I made myself even less attractive for friendship. However, I still had to be delivered from believing that I needed people to survive.

One glaring example came in my first year of college at the Historically Black College I attended. I was a member of the football team and it was customary after the football game for the players to go to a campus party. These parties convened weekly in the campus cafeteria and were loaded with students. Notwithstanding, it was one particular week early in the football season that I went to a party after the game and a fight broke out directly behind me. Those who know me would never believe this, but I was dancing at the time. Fights at parties were no big deal to be honest because at almost every party someone gets mad at someone for something. However, this fight was different. I was dancing within five feet of the people who were fighting and it lasted longer than expected. Then, to my surprise, I saw a gentleman take out a firearm and shoot directly at the ground. I was so close to him that the sparks from the gun almost touched my shoe. Please forgive me if I am wrong for this, but I didn't check on anyone, didn't see if anyone was hurt or even check if it was a fatal situation. I immediately climbed over people in pursuit of the closest exit. I ended up being the first one to get back to the dorm and I was in my room in less than three minutes. I wish at that moment that I had submitted an application for the NFL combine because I ran faster than I had ever run in my life. Now someone might be saying, "Well, what does this have to do with anything?" Well the entire reason why I attended the parties was to be accepted by the football team and the girls around campus. I knew before I went to those parties that I had no business going and for that matter any personal desire to go. I was never a person who enjoyed partying because it just was not for me. However, to please people I always went. That one decision to try to please people almost got me killed. From that moment until right now while I am writing this book, I have never stepped foot into another party or club. Why? Because I took that as a sign from God telling me that I had no business being in that environment because I knew that it was not productive.

Don't ever allow yourself to miss your purpose in the pursuit of pleasing people. Don't ever allow a temporary decision for a moment of pleasure to mess up your lifelong dreams or aspirations. The party that I attended was the situation that helped   me understand that I needed to be delivered from the need to be accepted. It was definitely not the easiest transition to make, but the decision to change ended up being one of the best decisions that I have ever made in life. Soon after that incident, my will was tested by Homecoming. Homecoming weekend is a much-anticipated weekend for many college students. During this week, my college hosted a top R&B artist and everyone was going to be there. My decision on Homecoming weekend marks a major moment in my decision for change. I decided to go to the library after the game and write papers. Now I know that sounds crazy, but it's true. I was ridiculed, talked about, ostracized, and badgered for this decision. Even during my trip up to the library, I was tested again because I had to press through the crowd, like the woman with the issue of blood in the Bible. Along the way, people were asking me if I would be at the party, but I had to ignore them to avoid being distracted. After finally making it out of the crowd and reaching the library, I had to encourage myself, knowing that I was making the right decision. I quickly realized that I was the only student in the library at the time; however, it was in that moment that I made a statement that I have lived by until this day. "What I do today will pay off in the end."

If you cultivate an attitude that does not depend

on people, you can do a lot of things by yourself. The funny axiom that my father used to say all the time was, "Sometimes the only decent conversation that you can have is with yourself." Too many times, the opinions of other people rule our lives and we need to be delivered from them. Now, I can do almost anything by myself. I frequently go to the movies, eat at restaurants, play golf, bowl, and even travel long distances by myself. Why? Because I realize I am really not alone. God is sitting there with me every step of the way. If you feel alone on the path of life or you are worried about being alone, know that you are in good company.

People who were alone:

Moses: When he encountered the burning bush
Jacob: When he wrestled with an angel until daybreak
Daniel: When he was locked inside the lion's den
Jesus: When he was in the Garden of Gethsemane
preparing for the crucifixion

What all of these great men in the Bible have in common is that they were never alone. God was with them during those moments that seemed frightening or scary because no one else was around. But He showed Himself strong and mighty through their lonely situations.

Don't misunderstand me. Loneliness is not what I am saying is the ultimate goal. However, what I am saying is to be alone if you have to, but connect with others if you can. Many times we do not connect with the right people, and our relationships end up being more detrimental than helpful.

A lack of comfort in our lonely places in life comes from not having a strong relationship with Christ. We must remind ourselves that the closer we get to Him, the more secure we will feel. He is the one there when no one else is around. He is the one that sticks closer than a brother. He is the one there to pick us up when everyone else has left us. He is the one that will never allow you to go so far that you step outside of His love and tender care. He is not like anyone else and he loves better than everyone else. He is the friend you have always wanted and the friend you ultimately will always need. The word ALONE is not a curse word; it's actually the best word at times because it sometimes takes being alone for Christ to truly get your undivided attention.

SECTION 3
Application

1. Set a specific time to reflect on your purpose in life. Have you discovered your WHY? If not, spend time this week in thought and prayer so that you can receive clarity on the plan and purpose for your life.

2. For one week, instead of checking social media, email, or the local news, try starting your day 15 minutes earlier with prayer. If you don't know what to say, or you have run out of words, sing a spiritual song. See if it makes a difference in the outcome of your day.

3. Examine your current friend circle. Do they represent a positive or negative influence in

your life? If negative, consider re-evaluating the level of friendship.

4. Challenge yourself to share a personal trial to triumph story with one person each week for a month. Take note of the impact made on you and the person you spoke to.

5. The next time someone asks you to do something that you know is wrong or something that you do not want to do, speak up and confront the person about the thought behind the suggested activity. This would be the perfect time to present the future problems that this activity will present or the opportunity for you to share why this activity does not benefit your personal advancement in life.

6. Consider reading the books, "All In" by Mark Batterson and "Not a Fan", by Kyle Idleman to get an understanding of why Christ must ultimately be your inspiration.

Final Words
CHAPTER 10
Setbacks May Come, But It's Okay

"When the greatest evangelist of the nineteenth century, D. L. Moody, was asked why he said he needed to be filled continually with the Holy Spirit, he replied, "Because I leak!" [1]

—*D. L. Moody*

I am grateful and thankful that you have made it to the last chapter of this book. I hope and pray that this read has been beneficial for you. However, while I know I have spoken a lot about what the Lord took me through to find life at my "dead end," I would be lying if I told you that I knew all of the answers, everything happened in order, and that I never had any setbacks. There were many days during this time when I reverted to some of my old ways. I have days like that even now. Many days, I just want to take a break from being on the grind of working. As a matter of fact, it is okay to take breaks. The problem comes when you start allowing yourself too many breaks and the breaks become more of a focus than the task at hand. In essence, we all have setbacks. That is why God sits there at your dead end to divinely direct you to where you need to be. Now some setbacks are more severe than others, but the concept stays the same. Identify the problem, implement a strategy for action mentally and physically, and find inspiration to stay focused along the way.

With that being said, I have developed several keys to remaining focused on this journey of discovery and change that I hope will help you stay on track.

1. Avoid crowds. During my time as a Maryland Terrapin football player, one player stood out. He separated himself by not following the crowd. He and I played the wide receiver position, so often we would be together running drills and routes, but he would always go the extra mile. Every drill and every play, he would run as fast and as hard as he

possibly could. This made me, the rest of the receivers, and sometimes the rest of the team mad because he would never slow up. This was especially true after the coaches punished the team because his running full speed exposed the fact that the rest of the team was running half speed. Regardless of how many times we asked him to join us in taking a break, he never did. He was simply determined not only to separate himself from the rest, but also to accomplish his end goal.

Whenever you are on a God-ordained path, few to no people are likely to agree with the new path that you have taken. This is when you have to rely on what Jesus taught during His Sermon on the Mount. According to Mathew 7, Jesus says that wide is the way of destruction and narrow is the gate to life. Essentially, a good indicator that you are on a good road is that you seemingly find yourself not needing to fight through swarms of people. The world, however, may convince you to believe otherwise. People want you to follow the road most taken because you will be with all of your friends, family, and acquaintances. I was always taught that whenever there is a crowd there is more than likely some form of confusion. We should be leery of paths in life that are popular because more than likely they will be the roads headed for destruction. As a result of that Maryland player's mentality, he has arguably accomplished more than many of the players on his team. Not only has he received a multi-million dollar contract and become one of the top-ranked receivers in the NFL, but he also was instrumental in bringing his NFL team a Super Bowl victory. And that great Maryland player's name is Torrey Smith. Don't join the crowd; set yourself apart.

2.   Don't base everything on creature comforts. When you are on a Divine assignment, earthly treasures may not always come immediately or at all. The Lord shares with us in His word that He shall supply all of our needs, not all of our wants. Therefore, we cannot always look for our heart's desires to be filled the second we make a good decision or the second we decide to follow a path that the Lord directed us to follow. This tends to be the frustrating part of following Christ because what might seem to be a necessity in our sight might be worthless in His. We might believe that we should have a certain income to fulfill the work of Christ, but in actuality we don't need as much as we think. If the Lord can use a little boy's two fish and five loaves of bread to feed thousands, then he can use anybody's $10,000 or $20,000 income to do his wonderful works.

3. Beware of sharing your dreams. If you are anything like me, you will be very excited once you make a decision that you know is God-ordained. You end up sharing your new decision with those who are your Christian friends or with those who have also made the same decision. Word to the wise: be very selective and discerning about the people with whom you share your future plans and decisions. Being premature in sharing about my new path bruised me. I had recently decided to start planning to go full time into ministry. I decided to share this with a gospel artist, who had made this decision earlier, was successful, and seemed happy about his decision. I spoke to the person specifically about the desire I had to quit my full-time comfortable job and move into full-time ministry. Ironically, the first thing out of that person's mouth was, "WHY!!!" So, I went on to say once more that the Lord had been speaking to me about my assignment in life and I pretty much ignored his reaction, thinking that he didn't fully understand me. But much to my shock and chagrin, his response was still the same. As a matter of fact, the person suggested that I not follow what the Lord revealed to me but continue traveling the world to gain more experience for my personal benefit. One of the worst decisions that I made was to prematurely share my dream because if I had been

weak-minded or unsure of the call of the Lord, this conversation would have destroyed me. This is what I want you to know: Be careful with whom you share your dreams. The person might seem to be the best person to share with because he or she is in the church, a Christian co-worker, or even a pastor. However, if you do not seek the Lord and be careful about those with whom you choose to share your dream, according to Ontario Green, "Your dream can quickly become a nightmare, when you tell the wrong people."

4. Develop a disciplined life. If I was forced to share one word that explains why I was able to conquer my early battle of mediocrity, that word would be discipline. Since those early periods, I have read many books about successful people and what they did to become successful. I found that almost every single person stated that their desire to develop daily routines and habits made the difference in their life. Living a disciplined life is about setting goals, objectives, or benchmarks that one will accomplish in a set period of time. In other words, doing exactly what you say you are going to do. If your objective is to wake up early and do something, then do it. Or if you have planned to start something within a week's time, then make sure you accomplish it. There is no greater disappointment to a person's future than a

goal planning session that will never be fulfilled. Otherwise those sessions are merely exercises in futility-lacking in substance. Leadership guru, John Maxwell states, "All great leaders have understood that their number one responsibility was for their own discipline ….. If they could not lead themselves, they could not lead others." [2]Furthermore, if we cannot trust ourselves, how can we expect others to trust us. If we cannot count on ourselves, how can we expect others to count on us. Therefore, we must commit to doing what we have planned so that we can build or restore confidence in ourselves. Developing a disciplined life may not be easy, but as John Maxwell says, it's the one thing that separates those that achieve great success from those who do not.

5. Get your daily dose of the Divine. In order for true fulfillment in life, Christ has to be apart of your daily life. Success will be short-lived if we try to take this journey without Him. For the truth of the matter is that we are nothing and will go nowhere without His direction. The Bible says in 2 Chronicles 7:14: "if my people, who are called by my name, will humble themselves and pray and seek my face and turn from their wicked ways, then I will hear from heaven and will forgive their sin and will heal their

land." My brothers and sisters, humility is the key to staying in constant connection with Christ. Regardless of personal stature or status, it makes no difference. In the sight of the Divine, humility has more to do with our will, than it does our possessions. Because a byproduct of giving up our will, will be a reprioritization of how we view our possessions. This is why the chronicler states that if we humble ourselves by relinquishing control of our lives, this is when we let go and give God the space to truly take over. It is central for us to grasp this concept because it will help us understand how we can stay on our path to destiny. If King David were here, I believe he would agree because he said in Psalm 121:1-2, "I lift up my eyes to the hills— where does my help come from? My help comes from the Lord, the Maker of heaven and earth." His help didn't come from his own hands, it didn't come from his neighbor's hands, it didn't come from a family member's hands. It is clear that his help came from above. The years spent guiding our own lives are over. We must go through life not looking down but looking up, because once our eyes are taken off of the Son, our lives are bound for failure. If we totally surrender our all to Him daily, we will experience in the end that we are right where we need to be.

I was talking one day with my closest friend. We are both Dallas Cowboys fans and were discussing the major differences between the team this year and previous years. In the 2014 season, the team was playing under the same coach that it had been for the last four and a half years. The head coach decided to call the plays in the role of the offensive coordinator and act as the head coach at the same time. During the head coach's tenure, the team had never made the playoffs or had a winning record. But in 2014, the Dallas Cowboys not only tied for the best regular season record in the NFL and won their divisional title, they also won a playoff game. This was something that had not been done in a long time. What was even more impressive about the season was that the team did not make any major additions to the player roster by signing star players to help turn the team around. They had a 12-4 record with most of the same players from the previous year. So, as we began to think, we discovered our answer. In the off-season, the team made the decision to hire a new offensive coordinator, a new play-caller who would take over all the play-calling responsibilities. The team's decision to turn over all play-calling responsibilities to someone else ended up turning their entire season around. That is all I am trying to tell you. Once you stop calling the plays for your life and turn them over to the One that has the ultimate plan, your life will start going in the direction it needs to go in and will never be the same. God bless.

Works Cited

Book Cover
- o "Torrey Smith." *NFL.com*. N.p., n.d. Web. 31 Mar. 2015. <http://www.nfl.com/player/torreysmith/2495459/profile>.

Acknowledgements
- o "Convocation Morning Worship Sermon with Otis Moss III." YouTube. YouTube, n.d. Web. 19 Jan. 2015.

Introduction
- o Charles, H. B. It Happens after Prayer: Biblical Motivation for Believing Prayer. N.p.: n.p., n.d. Print.
- o New Oxford American Dictionary. Copyright © 2010, 2013 by Oxford University Press

Chapter 1
- o Bell, James Stuart; Dawson, Anthony P. (2009-02-19).

From the Library of C. S. Lewis: Selections from Writers Who Influenced His Spiritual Journey (Writers' Palette Book) (Kindle Locations 1385-1386). Crown Religion/Business/Forum. Kindle Edition.

o Jay, Meg (2012-04-17). The Defining Decade: Why Your Twenties Matter—And How to Make the Most of Them Now (p. 44). Grand Central Publishing. Kindle Edition.

Chapter 2

o Dr. James R. McCartney (2013-06-29). Authentic Being: Dynamic Creativity (Kindle Locations 1230-1239). Xlibris. Kindle Edition.

Chapter 3

o Idleman, Kyle. Not a Fan: Becoming a Completely Committed Follower of Jesus. Grand Rapids, MI: Zondervan, 2011. Print.

Chapter 4

o "Making the Transition to Intentional Growth." John Maxwell on Leadership RSS. N.p., n.d. Web. 19 Jan. 2015.

o New Oxford American Dictionary. Copyright © 2010, 2013 by Oxford University Press

Chapter 5

- o "MLK." MLK. N.p., n.d. Web. 24 Jan. 2015. <http://assemblyseries.wustl.edu/past/MLK.html>.
- o "Making the Transition to Intentional Growth." *John Maxwell on Leadership RSS*. N.p., n.d. Web. 19 Jan. 2015. <http://johnmaxwellonleadership.com/2012/09/18/making-the-transition-to-intentional-growth/>.

Chapter 6

- o Maygers, Bryan. "Preachers of the Future: Three Sermons From Young Christians." *The Huffington Post*. TheHuffingtonPost.com, n.d. Web. 19 Jan. 2015 <http://www.huffingtonpost.com/2011/01/12/finding-their-voice-for-g_n_806758.html>.

Chapter 7

- o "The 2 Most Important Days In Your Life." *Inc.com*. N.p., n.d. Web. 16 Jan. 2015.<http://www.inc.com/dave-kerpen/leadership-the-most-important-days-in-your-life.html>.

Chapter 8

- o Idleman, Kyle. gods at War: Defeating The Idols That Battle For Your Heart. Mcleod Andrews. Zondervan, 2013. Audible.com. MP3
- o Idleman, Kyle. Not a Fan: Becoming a Completely

Committed Follower ofJesus. Grand Rapids, MI: Zondervan, 2011. Print.

Chapter 9

o *Poets.org.* Academy of American Poets, n.d. Web. 22 Jan. 2015. <http://www.poets.org/poetsorg/poem/road-not-taken>.

Chapter 10

o Charles, H. B. It Happens after Prayer: Biblical Motivation for Believing Prayer. N.p.:n.p.,n.d. Print.

o Maxwell, John (2007-04-10). Ultimate Leadership: 21 Irrefutable Laws, Developing the Leader Within You, 17 Indisputable Laws of Teamwork: 21 Irrefutable Laws, Developing the Leader Within You, 17 Indisputable Laws of Teamwork (Kindle Location 6022). Thomas Nelson. Kindle Edition.